THE
LIFE
Strategies
SELF-DISCOVERY
✦ JOURNAL ✦

THE

LIFE

Strategies

SELF-DISCOVERY
✦ JOURNAL ✦

*Finding What Matters
Most for You*

Phillip C. McGraw, Ph.D.

HYPERION
NEW YORK

Life is a journey. Luck comes only to those who have planned
carefully for it.

_____

_____

_____

_____

_____

_____

_____

_____

_____

_____

_____

_____

_____

_____

---　◆　---

Accept that life is unfair, and you will never feel like a victim.

_____

_____

_____

_____

_____

_____

_____

_____

_____

_____

_____

_____

_____

_____

—————————————— ◆ ——————————————

Life is a journey. Luck comes only to those who have planned carefully for it.

_____

_____

_____

_____

_____

_____

_____

_____

_____

_____

_____

_____

---------------------------- ◆ ----------------------------

Accept that life is unfair, and you will never feel like a victim.

_____

_____

_____

_____

_____

_____

_____

_____

_____

_____

_____

_____

_____

_____

_____

_____

Sometimes we need to step out of our own way. Be clear that *you* are not stopping yourself from succeeding.

_____

_____

_____

_____

_____

_____

_____

_____

_____

_____

_____

_____

_____

_____

Don't settle because you are afraid to take a stand. Making waves may be the only way to be heard.

_____

_____

_____

_____

_____

_____

_____

_____

_____

_____

_____

_____

_____

---◆---

Don't allow others to determine what is important to you. Yours is the voice that needs to be heard.

_____

_____

_____

_____

_____

_____

_____

_____

_____

_____

_____

_____

_____

_____

Forgiveness is not about the other person. It is about *you*.

_____

_____

_____

_____

_____

_____

_____

_____

_____

_____

_____

_____

_____

_____

Take ownership of your problems, and those who can help, will.

---◆---

If you adjust your focus and find a new set of tools, you *can* change your life.

_____

_____

_____

_____

_____

_____

_____

_____

_____

_____

_____

_____

_____

_____

Choose a goal you can control.

_____

_____

_____

_____

_____

_____

_____

_____

_____

_____

_____

_____

_____

_____

People who consistently win play the game with passion. They get excited about what they are doing.

_____

_____

_____

_____

_____

_____

_____

_____

_____

_____

_____

_____

_____

_____

An alternative approach can be a solution to your problems.
Begin by admitting you have new things to learn.

_____

_____

_____

_____

_____

_____

_____

_____

_____

_____

_____

_____

_____

_____

A sound strategy and a firm grip on the rules of the game will keep the competition at bay and life's walls from closing in on you.

_____

_____

_____

_____

_____

_____

_____

_____

_____

_____

_____

_____

_____

If you act, rather than react, you will be one step ahead of the crowd at all times.

If you are constantly reevaluating your behavior, then you are never just "going through" the motions of life.

_____

_____

_____

_____

_____

_____

_____

_____

_____

_____

_____

_____

You must understand your role in creating the results that are in your life. Learn how to choose better so you have better.

_____

_____

_____

_____

_____

_____

_____

_____

_____

_____

_____

_____

_____

———————————— ◆ ————————————

Express your goals in terms that can be measured, observed, and quantified.

_____

_____

_____

_____

_____

_____

_____

_____

_____

_____

_____

_____

_____

_____

_____

Connect the dots. See how the choices you made determined the outcome you didn't want or need.

_____

_____

_____

_____

_____

_____

_____

_____

_____

_____

_____

_____

_____

_____

———————————— ✦ ————————————

Pretending a problem doesn't exist is the fastest way to prolonging its presence in your life.

_____

_____

_____

_____

_____

_____

_____

_____

_____

_____

_____

_____

_____

Resolve to make choices with knowledge and information rather than ignorance and fear.

_____

_____

_____

_____

_____

_____

_____

_____

_____

_____

_____

_____

_____

Acknowledge those things you are most afraid of, and you will challenge your beliefs and inform your future.

_____

_____

_____

_____

_____

_____

_____

_____

_____

_____

_____

_____

_____

———————— ◆ ————————

Life cannot be lived in a vacuum. To avoid trouble, you must be aware of the world in which you live.

_____

_____

_____

_____

_____

_____

_____

_____

_____

_____

_____

_____

_____

_____

———————— ◆ ————————

Winning is relative. But needing a strategy to get to the finish line is universal.

_____

_____

_____

_____

_____

_____

_____

_____

_____

_____

_____

_____

_____

_____

A life that is energized by working toward your goals is infinitely more fulfilling than one in which you don't even understand what you're missing.

Avoiding problems can be just as painful and invasive as facing them head on.

_____

_____

_____

_____

_____

_____

_____

_____

_____

_____

_____

_____

_____

_____

On any given day, you've either won or lost. It's up to you to determine what kind of day you're going to have.

_____

_____

_____

_____

_____

_____

_____

_____

_____

_____

_____

_____

_____

_____

The days are long, but the years are short. Life passes by, whether you're living it or not.

---------------------◆---------------------

It's not about being "right or wrong." It's really about whether or not your choices are working for you.

_____

_____

_____

_____

_____

_____

_____

_____

_____

_____

_____

_____

_____

Winners don't care if anyone else thinks they are right!

_____

_____

_____

_____

_____

_____

_____

_____

_____

_____

_____

_____

_____

It's your time and your turn! Find the guts to face your fears and your flaws—the rewards will be endless.

_____

_____

_____

_____

_____

_____

_____

_____

_____

_____

_____

_____

You are worth any and all efforts it takes to find your truth and build a strategy for your success.

_____

_____

_____

_____

_____

_____

_____

_____

_____

_____

_____

_____

_____

You don't need more money or more time to make a plan. You can find any tools you need to build a strategy within yourself.

_____

_____

_____

_____

_____

_____

_____

_____

_____

_____

_____

_____

_____

If you refuse to reflect upon your behavior, you lose out on the chance to examine the issues undermining your success.

_____

_____

_____

_____

_____

_____

_____

_____

_____

_____

_____

_____

_____

_____

_____

_____

Figure out what makes people tick and how you can make it work for you.

_____

_____

_____

_____

_____

_____

_____

_____

_____

_____

_____

_____

_____

It's easy to tell those people who get it from those who don't. Those who do are enjoying life, and those who don't are frustrated and doing without.

When you don't understand the rules, you cannot play the game of life successfully.

_____

_____

_____

_____

_____

_____

_____

_____

_____

_____

_____

_____

_____

_____

—————————— ◆ ——————————

Be willing to learn new things so you are more equipped to make better choices and decisions.

_____

_____

_____

_____

_____

_____

_____

_____

_____

_____

_____

_____

_____

Existing is just getting from one day to the next. Living is exercising your learned skills, attitudes, and abilities with a sharp focus.

_____

_____

_____

_____

_____

_____

_____

_____

_____

_____

_____

_____

_____

Use your knowledge to positively affect your goal: having a life that is unique and rewarding.

_____

_____

_____

_____

_____

_____

_____

_____

_____

_____

_____

_____

_____

_____

The world is a social place. Your interactions with others affect everything you do.

_____

_____

_____

_____

_____

_____

_____

_____

_____

_____

_____

_____

_____

_____

Winners take action. It's that simple.

———————————— ◆ ————————————

Life changes the moment you understand how your behavior
is undermining your chances for a unique and rewarding life.

_____

_____

_____

_____

_____

_____

_____

_____

_____

_____

_____

_____

_____

_____

_____

---◆---

Mastery of how the game of life is played means that you can determine the outcome of your endeavors.

_____

_____

_____

_____

_____

_____

_____

_____

_____

_____

_____

_____

_____

_____

Change can only come with understanding of oneself.

———————————— ◆ ————————————

Knowing the rules, and having a plan, makes success less a mystery and more about efficiency.

_____

_____

_____

_____

_____

_____

_____

_____

_____

_____

_____

_____

_____

Question and challenge anything that doesn't make sense to you. Accept nothing on blind faith or because "it's the way things have always been done."

_____

_____

_____

_____

_____

_____

_____

_____

_____

_____

_____

_____

_____

Ask for advice, but be discriminating about whose input you accept.

People are often unfair or insensitive. Sadly, it seems the more successful you are, the more frequently this behavior is directed toward you.

———————————— ◆ ————————————

Before your life can change, you must pull over, park, and change directions.

_____

_____

_____

_____

_____

_____

_____

_____

_____

_____

_____

_____

_____

You don't need to experience the pain of failure to understand that it is something you wish to avoid.

_____

_____

_____

_____

_____

_____

_____

_____

_____

_____

_____

_____

_____

—————————— ◆ ——————————

Life is not a dress rehearsal. Start implementing your plan now!

_____

_____

_____

_____

_____

_____

_____

_____

_____

_____

_____

_____

_____

_____

Courage is the quality that those who honestly confront themselves all share.

_____

_____

_____

_____

_____

_____

_____

_____

_____

_____

_____

_____

_____

_____

Life is competitive. The clock is ticking and someone is keeping score.

———————————— ◆ ————————————

Don't underestimate the difficulty in figuring out what it is you truly want for your life.

_____

_____

_____

_____

_____

_____

_____

_____

_____

_____

_____

_____

_____

---◆---

If your life is to improve, it will be only because you choose to take action and make it happen.

_____

_____

_____

_____

_____

_____

_____

_____

_____

_____

_____

_____

_____

Truly successful people can float along consistently *and* weather the raging storms with skill and calm.

_____

_____

_____

_____

_____

_____

_____

_____

_____

_____

_____

_____

_____

_____

_____

You must truly know and understand those people you are trying to affect.

Once anger and bitterness enter your heart, they will exert a powerful influence on all your relationships.

_____

_____

_____

_____

_____

_____

_____

_____

_____

_____

_____

_____

_____

_____

Fear of rejection is universal.

People will perform for you when their self-esteem is enhanced by your actions.

———————— ◆ ————————

There is concern for oneself in almost every situation that we encounter.

People can only "hear" and absorb what they really understand.

_____

_____

_____

_____

_____

_____

_____

_____

_____

_____

_____

_____

_____

If you've determined that your choices are not working for you, forget about explaining why you made them. Just change them!

_____

_____

_____

_____

_____

_____

_____

_____

_____

_____

_____

_____

People naturally like and trust those who return these good feelings.

_____

_____

_____

_____

_____

_____

_____

_____

_____

_____

_____

_____

_____

All people, even those we consider to have great character, are capable of acting petty and small.

_____

_____

_____

_____

_____

_____

_____

_____

_____

_____

_____

_____

_____

—————————— ◆ ——————————

Become a student of human nature. We are all social animals.

_____

_____

_____

_____

_____

_____

_____

_____

_____

_____

_____

_____

_____

_____

Commit to paying attention and reflecting upon the actions and behaviors of those around you.

_____

_____

_____

_____

_____

_____

_____

_____

_____

_____

_____

_____

_____

_____

Learn how to listen to and influence yourself before you attempt to influence others.

_____

_____

_____

_____

_____

_____

_____

_____

_____

_____

_____

_____

_____

_____

When you've accepted the knowledge that comes with learning new things, you will take the guesswork out of your decision making.

_____

_____

_____

_____

_____

_____

_____

_____

_____

_____

_____

_____

_____

_____

The person you most need to work on is you. Maximize your positive behaviors, and minimize negative behavior patterns.

_____

_____

_____

_____

_____

_____

_____

_____

_____

_____

_____

_____

_____

To appreciate the importance of "getting it," consider the state in which you may now be living.

_____

_____

_____

_____

_____

_____

_____

_____

_____

_____

_____

_____

_____

Being misinformed is perhaps more dangerous than being ignorant.

Worse than lack of knowledge is thinking you know something when you really don't.

_____

_____

_____

_____

_____

_____

_____

_____

_____

_____

_____

_____

_____

You are accountable for all that you do. Good or bad, your life belongs only to you.

_____

_____

_____

_____

_____

_____

_____

_____

_____

_____

_____

_____

_____

It's simple. Your actions determine your outcomes—all of the time.

‹ ◆ ›

If you truly want change in your life, you must accept that you create your own experience. Then you can analyze how your choices have created the results you want to change.

_____

_____

_____

_____

_____

_____

_____

_____

_____

_____

_____

_____

_____

_____

Anger, pain, and frustration are all feelings you may own. Be aware that owning them means you are accountable for their presence in your life.

_____

_____

_____

_____

_____

_____

_____

_____

_____

_____

_____

_____

_____

———————— ✦ ————————

Face your truths and your life will take off.

_____

_____

_____

_____

_____

_____

_____

_____

_____

_____

_____

_____

_____

Successful people own and embrace their problems as well as their triumphs.

_____

_____

_____

_____

_____

_____

_____

_____

_____

_____

_____

_____

_____

———————————— ◆ ————————————

Being accountable for your problems also means understanding that their solutions lie within you, too.

_____

_____

_____

_____

_____

_____

_____

_____

_____

_____

_____

_____

_____

Don't waste time "trying on" other people's desires. Your time is better spent thinking about what your life strategy is going to be.

_____

_____

_____

_____

_____

_____

_____

_____

_____

_____

_____

_____

_____

---◆---

You have always been the architect of your own experience.

_____

_____

_____

_____

_____

_____

_____

_____

_____

_____

_____

_____

_____

_____

Focus on changing your behavior to get better results, rather than what anybody else is saying or doing to you.

_____

_____

_____

_____

_____

_____

_____

_____

_____

_____

_____

_____

_____

Once you accept that your experience and outcomes are a result of your behavior, you can purposefully choose to change what experience and outcomes you now create.

Real accountability requires an unflinching look at yourself. To do otherwise will only cripple your effectiveness and your quest for answers or solutions.

_____

_____

_____

_____

_____

_____

_____

_____

_____

_____

_____

_____

_____

_____

Beware the very human reaction to escape accountability. Responsibility is a heavy load and we often try to escape the burden.

_____

_____

_____

_____

_____

_____

_____

_____

_____

_____

_____

_____

Avoid placing accountability elsewhere. You will only stall your efforts toward becoming a successful person.

_____

_____

_____

_____

_____

_____

_____

_____

_____

_____

_____

_____

_____

———————◆———————

Blaming others for your problems is characteristic of failure.

_____

_____

_____

_____

_____

_____

_____

_____

_____

_____

_____

_____

_____

Each positive step you take will move you closer toward changing your life in a meaningful and positive way.

_____

_____

_____

_____

_____

_____

_____

_____

_____

_____

_____

_____

_____

_____

---◆---

It is more important to learn how to manage and control your own behavior than it is to understand how to control others.

_____

_____

_____

_____

_____

_____

_____

_____

_____

_____

_____

_____

_____

_____

As an adult, you have full control over how you react to events of the past.

_____

_____

_____

_____

_____

_____

_____

_____

_____

_____

_____

_____

_____

Your life experience is made up of the choices you make and the outcomes that accompany them each and every day.

_____

_____

_____

_____

_____

_____

_____

_____

_____

_____

_____

_____

_____

Life is not static. It's your choice . . . and your result.

_____

_____

_____

_____

_____

_____

_____

_____

_____

_____

_____

_____

_____

_____

Your thoughts also contribute to your experiences. Your thoughts will affect the consequences associated with them.

_____

_____

_____

_____

_____

_____

_____

_____

_____

_____

_____

_____

_____

_____

Every thought is accompanied by a physiological reaction. In this way, thoughts are also a part of your behavior.

_____

_____

_____

_____

_____

_____

_____

_____

_____

_____

_____

_____

_____

_____

A negative internal dialogue will create more obstacles undermining your chances for happiness and success.

_____

_____

_____

_____

_____

_____

_____

_____

_____

_____

_____

_____

_____

Focus on the decisions you make most frequently, and understand how these choices affect your life.

_____

_____

_____

_____

_____

_____

_____

_____

_____

_____

_____

_____

_____

_____

---◆---

Every day you make the very important choice of how you present and define yourself to other people.

_____

_____

_____

_____

_____

_____

_____

_____

_____

_____

_____

_____

_____

Beware that you "get what you give." The manner in which you engage people will determine how they respond to you.

_____

_____

_____

_____

_____

_____

_____

_____

_____

_____

_____

_____

_____

———————————— ◆ ————————————

Bring an element of urgency into your thinking and planning about what you want. Move with a sense of purpose toward naming and claiming what you want.

_____

_____

_____

_____

_____

_____

_____

_____

_____

_____

_____

_____

_____

_____

_____

Your behavior determines how others will react to you.

Take an honest look at the way you interact with others, and you will understand why the world responds to you as it does.

When you awake in the morning with the knowledge that you are living an honest life, you can face the day with optimism and anticipation.

_____

_____

_____

_____

_____

_____

_____

_____

_____

_____

_____

_____

_____

Be conscious of creating experiences you revel in, rather than those that bring you unhappiness or discomfort.

_____

_____

_____

_____

_____

_____

_____

_____

_____

_____

_____

_____

_____

The realization that our every thought and action involves choice means that we can begin to create our own minute-to-minute and day-to-day experience.

_____

_____

_____

_____

_____

_____

_____

_____

_____

_____

_____

_____

_____

_____

Change often means entering unknown territory. Be aware there is more than a little discomfort and fear that accompanies it.

_____

_____

_____

_____

_____

_____

_____

_____

_____

_____

_____

_____

_____

_____

Get up off your knowledge and do something different with your life.

_____

_____

_____

_____

_____

_____

_____

_____

_____

_____

_____

_____

_____

---◆---

You will ensure little security for your future if you fail to actively manage yourself between now and then.

_____

_____

_____

_____

_____

_____

_____

_____

_____

_____

_____

_____

_____

_____

_____

_____

In any relationship, you make the rules and define your boundaries.

_____

_____

_____

_____

_____

_____

_____

_____

_____

_____

_____

_____

_____

Adjust your attitude so that you are willing to try new things.
A mind open to experience leads to a fuller existence.

Recognizing that you are in a rut is only half the battle. Remember, however, that the longer you stay trapped in a painful lifestyle, the harder it will be to create a new one.

_____

_____

_____

_____

_____

_____

_____

_____

_____

_____

_____

_____

_____

Identify the payoffs that drive your behavior and that of others. Control the payoffs to control your life.

_____

_____

_____

_____

_____

_____

_____

_____

_____

_____

_____

_____

_____

It is often the behavior we most want to change that is the hardest to eliminate. Knowing what you need to do and how to do it are two very different things.

_____

_____

_____

_____

_____

_____

_____

_____

_____

_____

_____

_____

_____

_____

Change can come in either of two important ways: Start behaving positively *or* stop behaving negatively.

_____

_____

_____

_____

_____

_____

_____

_____

_____

_____

_____

_____

_____

---- ◆ ----

People don't care about your intentions. They care about your actions.

_____

_____

_____

_____

_____

_____

_____

_____

_____

_____

_____

_____

_____

_____

---◆---

When we interact without thinking, we shortchange the value
of our relationships.

_____

_____

_____

_____

_____

_____

_____

_____

_____

_____

_____

_____

_____

_____

_____

Don't mistake positive repetitive behavior for "automatic pilot." It's more likely you've determined that your actions are working well for you.

_____

_____

_____

_____

_____

_____

_____

_____

_____

_____

_____

_____

_____

Our behavior always results in some kind of payoff. Make sure yours is the payoff you're looking for.

_____

_____

_____

_____

_____

_____

_____

_____

_____

_____

_____

_____

_____

It is not always the case that the pattern of behavior we exhibit and the accompanying results are what we want to want.

_____

_____

_____

_____

_____

_____

_____

_____

_____

_____

_____

_____

_____

_____

Payoffs are the "currency" of life. Only you can determine what form of payoff is best for you.

_____

_____

_____

_____

_____

_____

_____

_____

_____

_____

_____

_____

_____

Don't look to find the reasons for your problems in others.
They are only inside you.

_____

_____

_____

_____

_____

_____

_____

_____

_____

_____

_____

_____

_____

An important step in understanding your behavior is figuring out *what you are getting out of what you are doing.* It may be obvious, or it may require some careful thought.

_____

_____

_____

_____

_____

_____

_____

_____

_____

_____

_____

_____

_____

---◆---

Payoffs can undermine your life strategy by being powerful enough to support behavior you do not consciously want.

_____

_____

_____

_____

_____

_____

_____

_____

_____

_____

_____

_____

Change is the result of identifying behaviors you want to eliminate, evaluating their payoffs, and then focusing on a different set of consequences.

_____

_____

_____

_____

_____

_____

_____

_____

_____

_____

_____

_____

_____

Winners arm themselves with the tools they need to succeed: strategies, time lines, and commitment.

_____

_____

_____

_____

_____

_____

_____

_____

_____

_____

_____

_____

_____

Take the time to identify the five most persistent, negative patterns in your life. When you understand the specific behavior that defines this pattern, why it doesn't work for you, and why the payoff causes you to continue, only then can you make a thoughtful, deliberate change.

Acceptance from the people we interact with is our number one need and biggest payoff.

_____

_____

_____

_____

_____

_____

_____

_____

_____

_____

_____

_____

_____

_____

When you choose the behavior, you choose the consequences.

_____

_____

_____

_____

_____

_____

_____

_____

_____

_____

_____

_____

_____

When you are controlled by fear, change becomes easier to avoid. When you face the possibility of rejection, you can participate in the decision to alter your behavior.

_____

_____

_____

_____

_____

_____

_____

_____

_____

_____

_____

_____

_____

For every habitual behavior, make sure the payoff isn't the comfort that comes from avoiding risk.

The path of least resistance rewards you with only false comfort and relief from the anxiety that accompanies reaching for something else.

_____

_____

_____

_____

_____

_____

_____

_____

_____

_____

_____

_____

_____

_____

———————————— ◆ ————————————

Look long and hard at the negative behaviors in your life. Only you are accountable for your day-to-day actions.

_____

_____

_____

_____

_____

_____

_____

_____

_____

_____

_____

_____

_____

_____

Everyone should have a break point where the need to change exceeds the payoff of comfort and security.

_____

_____

_____

_____

_____

_____

_____

_____

_____

_____

_____

_____

_____

———————————— ◆ ————————————

Exploring, instead of just accepting your payoffs, will put you in control of your own and others' behavior.

_____

_____

_____

_____

_____

_____

_____

_____

_____

_____

_____

_____

_____

Hatred, anger, and resentment eat away at the heart and soul of the person who carries them.

_____

_____

_____

_____

_____

_____

_____

_____

_____

_____

_____

_____

_____

Stop making excuses and start making results.

It is often easier to figure out what you *don't* want in your life than what you *do* want.

_____

_____

_____

_____

_____

_____

_____

_____

_____

_____

_____

_____

_____

---◆---

When you resolve to pursue your goals, there is no more room in your life for habit or rigidity.

_____

_____

_____

_____

_____

_____

_____

_____

_____

_____

_____

_____

_____

Taking ownership of your role in any situation is the only way you can begin to change your position.

_____

_____

_____

_____

_____

_____

_____

_____

_____

_____

_____

_____

_____

---------------------- ◆ ----------------------

Self-destructive behaviors need to be acknowledged before they gain momentum and become more resistant to change.

_____

_____

_____

_____

_____

_____

_____

_____

_____

_____

_____

_____

_____

When you commit to learning about others, you will be amazed to discover the many different things that motivate us.

_____

_____

_____

_____

_____

_____

_____

_____

_____

_____

_____

_____

_____

Thinking allows us to weigh which consequence we choose.

If you hope to have a winning life strategy, you have to be honest about where your life is right now.

_____

_____

_____

_____

_____

_____

_____

_____

_____

_____

_____

_____

_____

_____

Lying to yourself by omission is just as dangerous as manipulating your own truths.

◆

You must constantly challenge any limiting beliefs you hold on to. Living with them will undermine your chances for success.

_____

_____

_____

_____

_____

_____

_____

_____

_____

_____

_____

_____

_____

A life decision to risk reasonably and risk responsibly is often rewarded with security and success.

Controlling the payoff for any behavior affects the influence we have on our own and others' actions.

_____

_____

_____

_____

_____

_____

_____

_____

_____

_____

_____

_____

_____

Problems will not magically "work out" with time. Time only prolongs the negative consequences you are living with.

If you are honest with yourself, it is never too late and you are never too far gone to make changes.

_____

_____

_____

_____

_____

_____

_____

_____

_____

_____

_____

_____

_____

Admit what is not working in your life, and then set out to change it.

_____

_____

_____

_____

_____

_____

_____

_____

_____

_____

_____

_____

---------------------------- ◆ ----------------------------

Acknowledgment is an unvarnished, truthful confrontation
with yourself about what you and others in your life are doing
that is destructive to a peaceful and happy existence.

_____

_____

_____

_____

_____

_____

_____

_____

_____

_____

_____

_____

_____

Effecting change means rising to the level of absolute, brutal honesty with yourself.

_____

_____

_____

_____

_____

_____

_____

_____

_____

_____

_____

_____

_____

_____

---- ◆ ----

Once acknowledged, a problem becomes much more difficult to live with.

_____

_____

_____

_____

_____

_____

_____

_____

_____

_____

_____

_____

_____

Your emotional life is created by the choices you make. Make them well, and you will have what you want.

People who consistently win get what they want because they know what they want.

_____

_____

_____

_____

_____

_____

_____

_____

_____

_____

_____

_____

_____

Give yourself the gift of honesty and proceed with clarity.

_____

_____

_____

_____

_____

_____

_____

_____

_____

_____

_____

_____

_____

Abdicating responsibility for your actions leaves you behaving like a victim, with absolutely no control of your future.

Life rewards action.

_____

_____

_____

_____

_____

_____

_____

_____

_____

_____

_____

_____

_____

_____

You need to understand all the angles of your goal so you can sense when you are heading toward it and when you are drifting off your course.

_____

_____

_____

_____

_____

_____

_____

_____

_____

_____

_____

_____

_____

_____

Accountability just may help you get a leg up on the competition. You understand that no one can engineer your success but you.

_____

_____

_____

_____

_____

_____

_____

_____

_____

_____

_____

_____

_____

_____

———————————— ◆ ————————————

Negotiate your relationships from a position of strength and power. Fear and self-doubt have no place in your quest for change.

_____

_____

_____

_____

_____

_____

_____

_____

_____

_____

_____

_____

_____

---◆---

Acting in a purposeful, meaningful, and constructive manner will bring you superior results.

_____

_____

_____

_____

_____

_____

_____

_____

_____

_____

_____

_____

_____

_____

You are your greatest resource. Exploit and manage it well.

---◆---

Measure your quality of life based on *results*, not intentions.

_____

_____

_____

_____

_____

_____

_____

_____

_____

_____

_____

_____

_____

_____

_____

Evaluate yourself using the same measures the rest of the world is using. The bottom line is all about results!

_____

_____

_____

_____

_____

_____

_____

_____

_____

_____

_____

_____

_____

_____

Procrastination, the presence of mere intention, is the bane of human existence.

_____

_____

_____

_____

_____

_____

_____

_____

_____

_____

_____

_____

_____

Seize opportunity for change when it presents itself, and create opportunity where it does not exist already.

---------------------- ✦ ----------------------

Commitment is one of the most important steps in achieving success.

_____

_____

_____

_____

_____

_____

_____

_____

_____

_____

_____

_____

_____

_____

The pain that accompanies problems that go unacknowledged can only be remedied by admitting they exist in the first place.

_____

_____

_____

_____

_____

_____

_____

_____

_____

_____

_____

_____

_____

_____

Accepting accountability for your life behooves you to reevaluate any past behaviors in which you may have thought of yourself as a victim.

_____

_____

_____

_____

_____

_____

_____

_____

_____

_____

_____

_____

_____

_____

Until knowledge, awareness, insights, and understandings are translated into action, they are of no value.

_____

_____

_____

_____

_____

_____

_____

_____

_____

_____

_____

_____

_____

_____

Winners are people who have taken meaningful action, not just thought about the things they want to do.

_____

_____

_____

_____

_____

_____

_____

_____

_____

_____

_____

_____

_____

---◆---

Life will not change for you. You need to change to live it!

_____

_____

_____

_____

_____

_____

_____

_____

_____

_____

_____

_____

_____

People often behave for reasons other than those that are immediately apparent.

———————————— ◆ ————————————

Turn your pain into the motivation you need to make changes
to improve the quality of your life.

_____

_____

_____

_____

_____

_____

_____

_____

_____

_____

_____

_____

_____

Life rewards those who stay in the game. Quitting may come at the price of your hopes and dreams.

_____

_____

_____

_____

_____

_____

_____

_____

_____

_____

_____

_____

_____

———————— ✦ ————————

You must be careful not to wallow in the mediocrity you've become accustomed to. Stepping up to a quality existence will require conscious resolve.

Denial is insidious. It slowly kills any real chance you have of overcoming your problems.

_____

_____

_____

_____

_____

_____

_____

_____

_____

_____

_____

_____

_____

_____

———————————— ◆ ————————————

Your negative behavior does not have to define you forever.
Decide that you are worth the risk and that your dreams are
not to be sold out.

_____

_____

_____

_____

_____

_____

_____

_____

_____

_____

_____

_____

_____

You must demand to be treated well, or be ready to walk.

_____

_____

_____

_____

_____

_____

_____

_____

_____

_____

_____

_____

_____

_____

Life decisions, the ones you've made with a foundation of honesty and careful thought, anchor you and define who you are.

_____

_____

_____

_____

_____

_____

_____

_____

_____

_____

_____

_____

_____

_____

Be persistent in the pursuit of your life's goals. The effort alone will fill you with satisfaction and reward.

_____

_____

_____

_____

_____

_____

_____

_____

_____

_____

_____

_____

_____

The bad news about accountability is that the burden is on you. The good news is that the choices are all yours.

Winning doesn't just happen to people. On the other hand, losing is what happens when you are not making the choice to win.

_____

_____

_____

_____

_____

_____

_____

_____

_____

_____

_____

_____

Identify the filters through which you view the world. Acknowledge your history without being controlled by it.

_____

_____

_____

_____

_____

_____

_____

_____

_____

_____

_____

_____

_____

_____

You are the sole agent of change in your life. Lounging in the comfort zone can be hazardous to your health.

_____

_____

_____

_____

_____

_____

_____

_____

_____

_____

_____

_____

---------------------------◆---------------------------

Time is our most precious commodity—failing to take purposeful action wastes it away.

_____

_____

_____

_____

_____

_____

_____

_____

_____

_____

_____

_____

_____

---------------------------- ◆ ----------------------------

You are, by definition, unique. Don't allow others to define you or the meanings you assign to your experiences.

_____

_____

_____

_____

_____

_____

_____

_____

_____

_____

_____

_____

_____

When we blame our situation on past events, we allow our history to control and dictate our present and future.

_____

_____

_____

_____

_____

_____

_____

_____

_____

_____

_____

_____

_____

Being hesitant about pursuing new endeavors may be due more to fear than to any other reason.

We all view the world through our own filter of experience. Make sure you understand how that changes your view so you can compensate accordingly.

Our most distorted filter is the one through which we view
ourselves.

_____

_____

_____

_____

_____

_____

_____

_____

_____

_____

_____

_____

_____

The need for acceptance touches every one of us.

_____

_____

_____

_____

_____

_____

_____

_____

_____

_____

_____

_____

_____

_____

Our perceptions are rife with fixed beliefs: negative ideas so entrenched in our thinking that they have become part of the filter with which we view the world.

_____

_____

_____

_____

_____

_____

_____

_____

_____

_____

_____

_____

_____

_____

Express your goals in terms of specific events or behaviors.
Leave no room for confusion about what you desire.

_____

_____

_____

_____

_____

_____

_____

_____

_____

_____

_____

_____

_____

A limiting belief is a negative self-perception that you "know" is true and can therefore do nothing to change.

When you commit to measuring your own success in terms of results, you are entitled to evaluate others on those terms as well.

Search your mind and heart for the limiting beliefs that you carry with you from day to day.

_____

_____

_____

_____

_____

_____

_____

_____

_____

_____

_____

_____

_____

Explore how you perceive the world. You have the power to control your interpretations of and attitudes about your life.

_____

_____

_____

_____

_____

_____

_____

_____

_____

_____

_____

_____

_____

Lack of accountability results in a lack of understanding the results of your behavior. Refuse to own your behavior, and you will never improve your results.

_____

_____

_____

_____

_____

_____

_____

_____

_____

_____

_____

_____

_____

———————————— ◆ ————————————

Challenging the views you hold about yourself will leave you amazed to find a whole new perspective.

_____

_____

_____

_____

_____

_____

_____

_____

_____

_____

_____

_____

_____

Every experience changes and, hopefully, improves you.

_____

_____

_____

_____

_____

_____

_____

_____

_____

_____

_____

_____

_____

The results of your behavior occur on many levels of awareness. Be mindful of the power and subtleties of these different forms.

_____

_____

_____

_____

_____

_____

_____

_____

_____

_____

_____

_____

_____

_____

◆

Honesty is a powerful force in aiding change. Don't make a difficult task more so by refusing to assess what is really happening in your life.

_____

_____

_____

_____

_____

_____

_____

_____

_____

_____

_____

_____

_____

Let your perception be grounded in your present truths, not your past history.

_____

_____

_____

_____

_____

_____

_____

_____

_____

_____

_____

_____

_____

Identify the filters through which you view the world. Acknowledge your history without being controlled by it.

_____

_____

_____

_____

_____

_____

_____

_____

_____

_____

_____

_____

_____

Life is always full of problems to solve and challenges to be met.

_____

_____

_____

_____

_____

_____

_____

_____

_____

_____

_____

_____

_____

_____

---- ◆ ----

You must realize that your plan will alter and sometimes change along the way. Winners adapt to these new developments.

_____

_____

_____

_____

_____

_____

_____

_____

_____

_____

_____

_____

_____

To achieve success at all stages of life, you must actively manage your expectations along the way.

_____

_____

_____

_____

_____

_____

_____

_____

_____

_____

_____

_____

_____

_____

Offer yourself a performance evaluation of your life management abilities. Rating your own skills may give you insight into obstacles that need to be overcome.

_____

_____

_____

_____

_____

_____

_____

_____

_____

_____

_____

_____

_____

Solving others' problems means you are not spending time resolving your own.

_____

_____

_____

_____

_____

_____

_____

_____

_____

_____

_____

_____

_____

When you resolve the problems that plague you, you give a strong, healthy, peaceful self to those you love.

_____

_____

_____

_____

_____

_____

_____

_____

_____

_____

_____

_____

_____

_____

Holding on to your fear of the unknown can paralyze and debilitate you.

_____

_____

_____

_____

_____

_____

_____

_____

_____

_____

_____

_____

_____

When you allow unfinished emotional business to accumulate, it will end up dominating your very spirit.

_____

_____

_____

_____

_____

_____

_____

_____

_____

_____

_____

_____

_____

_____

Effective life managers identify their frustration and take time out to deal with it directly.

_____

_____

_____

_____

_____

_____

_____

_____

_____

_____

_____

_____

_____

_____

Insist on getting closure in your life. Deal with your issues and then close the book on the problem or the pain you felt.

_____

_____

_____

_____

_____

_____

_____

_____

_____

_____

_____

_____

_____

_____

A person of substance honors his agreements, both large and small.

---- ◆ ----

Sometimes a payoff that seems to be working for you is really the path of least resistance. In that case, it's really not a payoff at all.

_____

_____

_____

_____

_____

_____

_____

_____

_____

_____

_____

_____

_____

Broken agreements are like boulders in front of and behind you on the road of life.

_____

_____

_____

_____

_____

_____

_____

_____

_____

_____

_____

_____

_____

You get what you give. If you hand out anger and bitterness, do not expect love and acceptance in return.

Carrying around anger erodes your quality of life.

_____

_____

_____

_____

_____

_____

_____

_____

_____

_____

_____

_____

_____

Negative behavior repeats only when the payoff is significant to you in some way.

_____

_____

_____

_____

_____

_____

_____

_____

_____

_____

_____

_____

_____

_____

When your sense of security involves living to avoid change, pain, and intimacy, it is not living at all.

_____

_____

_____

_____

_____

_____

_____

_____

_____

_____

_____

_____

_____

The most powerful and self-destructive emotions—hate, anger, and resentment—are the result of how you perceive yourself to have been hurt by those you love.

_____

_____

_____

_____

_____

_____

_____

_____

_____

_____

_____

_____

_____

Lives full of energy and purpose are managed with design and commitment.

_____

_____

_____

_____

_____

_____

_____

_____

_____

_____

_____

_____

_____

_____

Your life is your own special project—you need to attack your problems and make changes with a sense of urgency and significance.

_____

_____

_____

_____

_____

_____

_____

_____

_____

_____

_____

_____

_____

You must break down your goal into measurable steps so that you don't just expect it to "happen."

_____

_____

_____

_____

_____

_____

_____

_____

_____

_____

_____

_____

_____

---- ◆ ----

"Lucky" people haven't settled for just okay.

_____

_____

_____

_____

_____

_____

_____

_____

_____

_____

_____

_____

_____

Accountability does not imply intent. It says only that you acknowledge behavior as your responsibility.

_____

_____

_____

_____

_____

_____

_____

_____

_____

_____

_____

_____

_____

_____

Study and dissect your mistakes so you can avoid repeating them.

A strategy requires courage, commitment, and energy in order to succeed.

If you are being treated undesirably, reflect on what you may be doing to elicit or allow that treatment.

_____

_____

_____

_____

_____

_____

_____

_____

_____

_____

_____

_____

_____

_____

———————————— ✦ ————————————

A life decision is one of conviction, made from the heart, and something you live by all of the time.

_____

_____

_____

_____

_____

_____

_____

_____

_____

_____

_____

_____

_____

_____

Dreams are all about an objective that is merely longed for.
Goals involve a strategic plan for getting there.

_____

_____

_____

_____

_____

_____

_____

_____

_____

_____

_____

_____

_____

_____

Writing down your life decisions will enhance your awareness
of the importance of these convictions.

_____

_____

_____

_____

_____

_____

_____

_____

_____

_____

_____

_____

_____

_____

Would you retain a manager who wasn't getting high-quality results? You are the manager of your own life, and if you don't know how you're doing, then it is time to reevaluate your skills.

_____

_____

_____

_____

_____

_____

_____

_____

_____

_____

_____

_____

_____

_____

_____

_____

_____

_____

Life is anything but a success-only journey.

Evaluate how you are managing your life as if you were evaluating an employee. Step back for some needed objectivity and assess how well you are running the show.

_____

_____

_____

_____

_____

_____

_____

_____

_____

_____

_____

_____

_____

_____

_____

Identify important episodes in your life when you felt you were victimized. Allow your knowledge of accountability to help you understand what role you played in your unwanted results.

_____

_____

_____

_____

_____

_____

_____

_____

_____

_____

_____

_____

_____

_____

It is human nature to resist what is new or what we don't understand. But with conscious resolve, you can overcome that human truth.

_____

_____

_____

_____

_____

_____

_____

_____

_____

_____

_____

_____

_____

_____

You must constantly reevaluate the standards you've set for yourself so that you are aiming neither too high nor too low.

_____

_____

_____

_____

_____

_____

_____

_____

_____

_____

_____

_____

_____

Choosing to hold on to hate, anger, or resentment will result in negative energy having influence over your life.

_____

_____

_____

_____

_____

_____

_____

_____

_____

_____

_____

_____

_____

_____

_____

_____

You must ask for excellence from yourself so that you can drive your life on, not idle away in the passenger seat.

_____

_____

_____

_____

_____

_____

_____

_____

_____

_____

_____

_____

_____

Make a decision now about what you will *demand* from yourself and what you are willing to *accept* from yourself.

_____

_____

_____

_____

_____

_____

_____

_____

_____

_____

_____

_____

_____

_____

_____

_____

Expect that when you ask more of yourself and from your partner, there will be a resistance to changing the status quo. *No one* likes change.

_____

_____

_____

_____

_____

_____

_____

_____

_____

_____

_____

_____

Your emotional life is created by the choices you make. Make them well, and you will have what you want.

_____

_____

_____

_____

_____

_____

_____

_____

_____

_____

_____

_____

_____

Relationships are mutually defined. Each participant contributes importantly to the negotiations involved.

———————— ◆ ————————

As your life begins to flow more smoothly, look back on the changes you have made with pride and satisfaction.

_____

_____

_____

_____

_____

_____

_____

_____

_____

_____

_____

_____

_____

If you remain status quo, you will achieve status quo. If you behave differently, your outcomes will be different.

_____

_____

_____

_____

_____

_____

_____

_____

_____

_____

_____

_____

_____

_____

You must resolve to work harder and work smarter. Demand more from yourself in every area, across the board.

_____

_____

_____

_____

_____

_____

_____

_____

_____

_____

_____

_____

_____

Hatred, anger, and resentment are absolutely incompatible with peace, joy, and relationships.

_____

_____

_____

_____

_____

_____

_____

_____

_____

_____

_____

_____

_____

Begin each day with the question: "What can I do *today* to make my life better?" Ask it, answer it, and then do it every day.

_____

_____

_____

_____

_____

_____

_____

_____

_____

_____

_____

_____

_____

Consciously stepping up your efforts to achieve excellence should be a cornerstone for the foundation of your life strategy.

You are your own most important resource for making your life work. Manage your interior self skillfully and it will reflect well upon your overall existence.

_____

_____

_____

_____

_____

_____

_____

_____

_____

_____

_____

_____

_____

Responsibility isn't just about making the right decisions. Sometimes it is about making right a wrong decision you have made.

_____

_____

_____

_____

_____

_____

_____

_____

_____

_____

_____

_____

_____

Don't let others deter you from understanding accountability. Maintain a sharp focus on those things that will truly change your life.

_____

_____

_____

_____

_____

_____

_____

_____

_____

_____

_____

_____

_____

Poor choices test your maturity and resolve and your commitment to implement change in your life.

_____

_____

_____

_____

_____

_____

_____

_____

_____

_____

_____

_____

_____

_____

You are managing many lives. Your emotional, social, spiritual, and physical lives must be cared for with knowledge and a sense of purpose.

_____

_____

_____

_____

_____

_____

_____

_____

_____

_____

_____

_____

_____

---------------------------- ◆ ----------------------------

You must renegotiate your relationships to have what you want.

_____

_____

_____

_____

_____

_____

_____

_____

_____

_____

_____

_____

_____

_____

You are an active participant in defining your relationships with others. Your reactions to their behavior will determine what choices they make in the future.

_____

_____

_____

_____

_____

_____

_____

_____

_____

_____

_____

_____

_____

Knowledge is power, but the lack of it can be harmful. Resolve to make gathering information about yourself and those around you a priority.

_____

_____

_____

_____

_____

_____

_____

_____

_____

_____

_____

_____

_____

A life decision to risk reasonably and risk responsibly is often rewarded with security and success.

The universe rewards action and leaves the inactive wondering why they keep missing out on life.

_____

_____

_____

_____

_____

_____

_____

_____

_____

_____

_____

_____

---- ◆ ----

Don't blame your partner if you are dissatisfied with your relationship. You own 50 percent of it!

_____

_____

_____

_____

_____

_____

_____

_____

_____

_____

_____

_____

_____

_____

———————————— ◆ ————————————

You teach people how far they can push you by either rewarding their destructive relationship behavior or passively allowing them to persist in that behavior.

_____

_____

_____

_____

_____

_____

_____

_____

_____

_____

_____

_____

_____

_____

Winners have no room in their lives for deception. They "tell it like it is" to themselves and others.

_____

_____

_____

_____

_____

_____

_____

_____

_____

_____

_____

_____

_____

You must make a life decision that you would rather be well by yourself than sick with someone else.

_____

_____

_____

_____

_____

_____

_____

_____

_____

_____

_____

_____

_____

When you forgive, you seize the power to rise above your pain.
You deserve no less.

_____

_____

_____

_____

_____

_____

_____

_____

_____

_____

_____

_____

_____

Accountability just may help you get a leg up on the competition. You understand that no one can engineer your success but you.

_____

_____

_____

_____

_____

_____

_____

_____

_____

_____

_____

_____

_____

Don't just talk about change—act. When you don't follow through, your statements and declarations will not be taken seriously.

_____

_____

_____

_____

_____

_____

_____

_____

_____

_____

_____

_____

_____

Do not compromise your relationship standards for anyone.
Doing so means selling yourself out.

_____

_____

_____

_____

_____

_____

_____

_____

_____

_____

_____

_____

_____

Understanding and accepting that you view the world through your own unique filters takes you one step closer to understanding your reality.

_____

_____

_____

_____

_____

_____

_____

_____

_____

_____

_____

_____

_____

_____

Recognize your limiting beliefs so that you can counteract those thoughts as soon as they occur.

_____

_____

_____

_____

_____

_____

_____

_____

_____

_____

_____

_____

_____

_____

———————— ◆ ————————

Have an open and honest conversation with yourself about the
status of any relationship you seek to change.

_____

_____

_____

_____

_____

_____

_____

_____

_____

_____

_____

_____

_____

_____

It is often hardest to "unlearn" ideas before accepting a new kind of knowledge and understanding.

_____

_____

_____

_____

_____

_____

_____

_____

_____

_____

_____

_____

_____

_____

Guilt is powerful, destructive, and paralyzing. No one makes progress when burdened with shame.

Ask people to do for you only what you know you can and are willing to do for them.

_____

_____

_____

_____

_____

_____

_____

_____

_____

_____

_____

_____

Don't take on someone else's baggage if you're still carrying some of your own.

_____

_____

_____

_____

_____

_____

_____

_____

_____

_____

_____

_____

_____

The bad news about accountability is that the burden is on you. The good news is that the choices are all yours.

_____

_____

_____

_____

_____

_____

_____

_____

_____

_____

_____

_____

_____

Forgiveness is really about taking power from those who have hurt you.

_____

_____

_____

_____

_____

_____

_____

_____

_____

_____

_____

_____

_____

_____

Carrying the burden of hatred comes at a high price. It will fatally wound your heart and mind.

_____

_____

_____

_____

_____

_____

_____

_____

_____

_____

_____

_____

_____

Coasting through a familiar situation is often the result of conscious choices you've made and hard work you've done in the past.

_____

_____

_____

_____

_____

_____

_____

_____

_____

_____

_____

_____

_____

—————————◆—————————

Forgiveness is all about preserving control over your own emotional state.

_____

_____

_____

_____

_____

_____

_____

_____

_____

_____

_____

_____

_____

_____

Allow those whom you have locked in a bond of anger to go free. Your own freedom is at stake.

_____

_____

_____

_____

_____

_____

_____

_____

_____

_____

_____

_____

_____

To know someone, you must look beyond the mask that person puts on to greet the world.

_____

_____

_____

_____

_____

_____

_____

_____

_____

_____

_____

_____

_____

The only thing worse than being hurt by someone you love is nurturing that pain even after he or she has gone.

_____

_____

_____

_____

_____

_____

_____

_____

_____

_____

_____

_____

_____

---◆---

You must know exactly what you want before you can step up
and claim it.

_____

_____

_____

_____

_____

_____

_____

_____

_____

_____

_____

_____

_____

Understanding the rules of life can make you more competitive and less open to others who can block your success or control you in any way.

_____

_____

_____

_____

_____

_____

_____

_____

_____

_____

_____

_____

_____

Choosing solid, reliable teachers will ensure that you are only increasing your store of personal knowledge.

_____

_____

_____

_____

_____

_____

_____

_____

_____

_____

_____

_____

_____

—————————— ◆ ——————————

Being wrong or misguided about your needs and desires is
even worse than not knowing them at all.

_____

_____

_____

_____

_____

_____

_____

_____

_____

_____

_____

_____

_____

Opportunities have a shelf life that can and will expire. The clock is ticking and you need to act.

_____

_____

_____

_____

_____

_____

_____

_____

_____

_____

_____

_____

_____

_____

When you know your goals, you will recognize which choices support them and which do not.

_____

_____

_____

_____

_____

_____

_____

_____

_____

_____

_____

_____

_____

You are not a victim, but a leader in creating the situations and emotions that are present in your life.

_____

_____

_____

_____

_____

_____

_____

_____

_____

_____

_____

_____

_____

_____

◆

Be bold, yet realistic. The most you'll ever get is what you ask for.

_____

_____

_____

_____

_____

_____

_____

_____

_____

_____

_____

_____

_____

_____

———————— ◆ ————————

Take stock of who and where you are in life and set your goals
accordingly.

_____

_____

_____

_____

_____

_____

_____

_____

_____

_____

_____

_____

_____

_____

Be willing to step up to the plate and say, "I'm up." It's your turn.

_____

_____

_____

_____

_____

_____

_____

_____

_____

_____

_____

_____

_____

If you believe that you deserve the things you want, you will have the strength to claim your prize.

_____

_____

_____

_____

_____

_____

_____

_____

_____

_____

_____

_____

_____

No one else is going to get the job done for you. If you don't seize the moment, the moment disappears.

_____

_____

_____

_____

_____

_____

_____

_____

_____

_____

_____

_____

_____

If you are unable or unwilling to acknowledge your negative characteristics, then there is no hope of changing them.

_____

_____

_____

_____

_____

_____

_____

_____

_____

_____

_____

_____

_____

You have the right to be just who you are, as long as your uniqueness is not at the expense of another's dignity or respect.

_____

_____

_____

_____

_____

_____

_____

_____

_____

_____

_____

_____

_____

———————————— ◆ ————————————

Stop and take a look around. You may be closer to greatness than you ever imagined.

_____

_____

_____

_____

_____

_____

_____

_____

_____

_____

_____

_____

_____

Resolve to believe that your desires are valid and real and that, when your time comes, you will claim your right to them.

◆

Effectively manage yourself, and that knowledge will help you
manage others.

_____

_____

_____

_____

_____

_____

_____

_____

_____

_____

_____

_____

_____

_____

Your behavior determines a pattern that defines you in the eyes of the world, determines other people's reactions to you, and, therefore, determines your experiences of the world.

_____

_____

_____

_____

_____

_____

_____

_____

_____

_____

_____

_____

_____

_____

Assign a time line to your goal. A schedule of achievement will keep your goal from dissolving into only a dream.

_____

_____

_____

_____

_____

_____

_____

_____

_____

_____

_____

_____

_____

_____

_____

—————————— ◆ ——————————

Make role models of those people you know whose strategies
and characteristics are generating great results.

_____

_____

_____

_____

_____

_____

_____

_____

_____

_____

_____

_____

_____

_____

_____

Winners are responsible risk-takers. They step out of their comfort zone armed with information and determination.

Create accountability for your progress toward your goal. Each step ahead can be counted as a success.

_____

_____

_____

_____

_____

_____

_____

_____

_____

_____

_____

_____

_____

_____

_____

You must be willing to challenge *everything* you may have previously treated with automatic resistance.

_____

_____

_____

_____

_____

_____

_____

_____

_____

_____

_____

_____

_____

---------------------------------- ✦ ----------------------------------

Accountability never changes. It will follow you through all the stages of your life.

_____

_____

_____

_____

_____

_____

_____

_____

_____

_____

_____

_____

_____

Each positive step you take will move you closer toward changing your life in a meaningful and everlasting way.

_____

_____

_____

_____

_____

_____

_____

_____

_____

_____

_____

_____

_____

_____

Study and dissect your mistakes so you can avoid repeating them.

_____

_____

_____

_____

_____

_____

_____

_____

_____

_____

_____

_____

_____

_____

A negative, self-effacing internal dialogue will badly affect the way you interact with the world.

_____

_____

_____

_____

_____

_____

_____

_____

_____

_____

_____

_____

_____

_____

Study and analyze your success so you can repeat the behavior that has brought you positive results.

_____

_____

_____

_____

_____

_____

_____

_____

_____

_____

_____

_____

_____

_____

Winners take action. It's that simple.